# Mi comunidad

Lee Aucoin

POST OFFICE
AND COURT HOUSE

LETTER CARRIER

Medical
Center

Accident & Emergency D
AMBULANCE
AMBULANCE

Public
Library
LIB

RARY

Kids Around the World

POLICE

POLICE
110 SOUTH 5TH AVE.
POLICE DEPARTMENT
POLICE DEPARTMENT
DIAL 911
POLICE

FIRE DEPART

MENT
27

227
MINI SUPER MA
The Guardian
DAILY EXPRESS
Daily Mail
PARADE TODAY

KET
COST
WELCOME TO
JEWEL INTERNET CAFE
1 per hour